Cornerstones of Freedom

The Story of
THE NINETEENTH AMENDMENT

By R. Conrad Stein

Illustrated by Keith Neely

CHILDRENS PRESS, CHICAGO

Library of Congress Cataloging in Publication Data

Stein, R. Conrad.
  The Story of the Nineteenth Amendment.

  (Cornerstones of freedom)
  Summary: A history of the movement to grant
women the right to vote in the United States,
which culminated in the nineteenth amendment
to the Constitution in 1920 that permitted them
to do so.
  1. Women—Suffrage—United States—Juvenile
literature. [1. Women—Suffrage] I. Neely,
Keith R. ill. II. Title. III. Series.
KF4895.Z9S73   342.73'072   82-4419
ISBN 0-516-04639-X   347.30272   AACR2

Copyright© 1982 by Regensteiner Publishing Enterprises, Inc.
All rights reserved. Published simultaneously in Canada.
Printed in the United States of America.
  3 4 5 6 7 8 9 10 R 91 90 89 88 87 86 85 84

The Nineteenth Amendment to the United States Constitution reads: "The right of the citizens of the United States to vote shall not be denied or abridged by the United States or any State on account of sex." Simply stated, that means women are permitted to vote. Today it is difficult to imagine a time when women could not vote. But just a little more than sixty years ago, voting rights for women was a very emotional issue. Heated discussions of the subject often ended in street brawls.

Women won the right to vote only after a long, bitter struggle. The roots of that struggle lie deep in American history.

During the time the United States belonged to Great Britain, a few colonies allowed women who were property owners to vote in certain elections. Those elections were concerned mainly with local issues such as road repairs and school taxes.

Some women objected to being denied the vote. As early as 1647, a woman named Margaret Brent demanded a "place and a voice" in the Maryland Assembly. Her demand was rejected by the all-male council. Another woman, Anne Hutchinson, spoke up for women's rights in Massachusetts Colony. At the time, Massachusetts was dominated by the stern Puritans. Because she spoke out, Anne Hutchinson was banished from the colony.

Only a few women dared to demand their rights in the colonial United States. By the early 1800s, women had lost even their very limited voting privileges. Then, in the 1820s and 1830s, an issue emerged that roused American women. That issue was the growing protest against slavery.

American women joined the fight against slavery for several reasons. The most obvious reason was the outrage they felt that some people were born slaves while others were born free. Also, many of the women who fought slavery were Quakers. The Quakers were enemies of slavery, and their church was the only major church that recognized the rights of women. Finally, it could be said that nineteenth-century American women felt an identity with the slaves. At that time, women lived almost like slaves. Their fathers, husbands, and brothers were their masters.

To fight slavery, many women became agents in the Underground Railroad. The Underground Railroad was a secret organization whose men and women members risked their lives to help slaves escape to freedom. Other women joined abolitionist societies. Abolitionists were people who wanted to end (abolish) slavery in the United States.

The struggle for women's rights was born from the anti-slavery movement. One young woman who fought slavery and later led the women's rights movement was Elizabeth Cady Stanton.

Elizabeth Cady grew up in Johnstown, New York. She was the daughter of a well-to-do judge. When Elizabeth was ten, she overheard her father talking to a woman who had come to him in tears. The woman complained that her drunken husband was about to sell the farm she had inherited from her parents. Judge Cady told the woman he could do nothing. The law gave the man the right to sell any property owned by the family. Ten-year-old Elizabeth was shocked by the unfairness of the law. Deciding to "cut" the law out of the books, she took a pair of scissors from her desk. Fortunately for Judge Cady, he was able to stop his daughter before she did any damage to his law books.

Elizabeth later married a handsome, anti-slavery activist named Henry Stanton. In those days a wife vowed to love, honor, and *obey* her husband. But Elizabeth instructed the parson to remove the word "obey" from the wedding vows.

For their honeymoon, Henry and Elizabeth sailed to England to attend a world anti-slavery convention. At the convention Elizabeth was introduced to a woman named Lucretia Mott. Mrs. Mott was twenty-two years older than Mrs. Stanton. But when those two met, a new movement began.

Lucretia Mott had been born in Massachusetts to a devout Quaker family. She and her husband were both agents on the Underground Railroad. Lucretia Mott also had founded the first female anti-slavery society. She had been an early supporter of women's rights. "Mrs. Mott was to me an entirely new revelation of womanhood," wrote Elizabeth Stanton. "I sought every opportunity to be at her side, and continually plied her with questions."

The two women agreed to work together for women's rights in the United States. Each brought special talents to the cause. Mrs. Stanton was a gifted writer who wrote powerful letters and speeches. Mrs. Mott became the spiritual leader of the movement.

In June of 1848, Elizabeth Stanton, Lucretia Mott, and others met in the town of Seneca Falls, New York. They formed the famous Seneca Falls Convention. It was the first tiny step in the long march for women's rights.

At the Seneca Falls Convention, sixty-eight women and thirty-two men signed a statement. Part of the statement was based on the American Declaration of Independence. It said, "We hold these truths to be self-evident: that all men *and women* are created equal...." The statment continued: "The history of mankind is a history of repeated injuries and usurpations on the part of men toward women, having in direct object the establishment of an absolute tyranny over her."

The convention demanded that equal education be provided for women. Women also wanted the right to teach, to preach, and to earn a living. How would they secure those rights? "It is the sacred duty of the women of this country to secure to themselves their sacred right to the elective franchise." That meant women must have suffrage. Suffrage means the right to vote.

Calling for woman suffrage was the most radical demand made by the Seneca Falls Convention. Some women thought that asking for the vote was going too far. But Elizabeth Stanton insisted that the right to vote was a fundamental right of all citizens of the United States.

After the Seneca Falls Convention, more women joined Elizabeth Stanton and Lucretia Mott. One of them was Amelia Jenks Bloomer. She urged women to wear a costume of knee-length skirts and ankle-length pantaloons. The new outfit came to be called "bloomers." For a while, bloomers became the uniform of the women's rights workers. The workers were sometimes called "bloomer girls." Amelia Bloomer also is remembered for introducing Elizabeth Stanton to a dynamic young woman named Susan B. Anthony.

Miss Anthony, born to a Quaker family, had grown up in the fight against slavery. She became active in the fight for women's rights when she was a schoolteacher and discovered that a male teacher

ELIZABETH CADY
STANTON

LUCRETIA MOTT

in her school was being paid forty dollars a month. She was paid only ten. Susan Anthony quickly formed a close friendship with Elizabeth Stanton. Miss Anthony was a superb organizer and a tireless worker. She brought her inexhaustible energy to the long campaign.

Lucy Stone was another early women's rights leader. She was an excellent speaker. Lucy Stone could have displayed her speaking talent while still in college, but anti-woman customs silenced her. Lucy graduated from Ohio's Oberlin College in 1847. She wrote an essay so brilliant that the Oberlin professors decided to use it during her graduation ceremony. But Lucy Stone would not be permitted to read her essay to the public. In those days, public speaking was not thought to be a proper activity for

SUSAN B. ANTHONY

LUCY STONE

a woman. Instead, the essay would be read by one of her professors. Lucy was so angry that she refused to have it read at all.

The famous four of American women's rights became Elizabeth Stanton, Lucretia Mott, Susan B. Anthony, and Lucy Stone. Each brought her special talents to the movement. Elizabeth Stanton was the writer, Lucy Stone the speaker, Susan B. Anthony the organizer, and Lucretia Mott the spiritual leader. They often disagreed as to how to achieve their goals. But they did agree that women must have rights. And the most fundamental of those rights was the right to vote.

Gaining the vote was an almost impossible goal for those pioneers of women's rights. To attain the vote, women needed political power. But to get political power they needed the vote. Trying to gain the vote without having the vote would be difficult indeed.

Despite the odds, the women began their struggle. They made speeches, circulated petitions, and called on political leaders.

Immediately the women made enemies. Old-line politicians, who resisted any kind of change, opposed voting rights for women. Newspapers were hostile toward the demand for woman suffrage. Some newspapers called the movement "the battle of the petticoats." An editorial in the Springfield Massachusetts *Republican* warned Lucy Stone: "You she-hyena, don't you come here." Many churches opposed voting rights for women. A columnist in a paper called the *Gospel Advocate* wrote: "Everyone knows that men and women are not equal in all things. I do not believe that good women *want* the ballot; but even if they did, the question which man must determine is not affected by what women *want*, but by what they *ought* to have."

The most powerful opponents of woman suffrage were men. Some men wanted to deny women the vote because they did not want to share their power. But the attitudes of most men simply reflected the times. "The prerogative of man is to command. . . the prerogative of woman is to obey." Those lines came from the Charles Dickens novel *Oliver Twist.* The attitude that men should command was shared by most men of the nineteenth century, and by most women as well.

Early in the movement's history it was difficult to convince women to stand up for their rights. Many women clung to the ancient belief that men should be their masters. Elizabeth Stanton wrote about what often happened when a women's rights worker knocked on a housewife's door: "They would gruffly tell her they had all the rights they wanted, or rudely shut the door in her face, leaving her to stand outside, petition in hand. . . as if she were asking for alms for herself." The woman suffrage leaders often found it difficult even to speak in public. In the mid-1800s a woman standing on a platform addressing a crowd was a shocking sight. Like children, women were supposed to be seen but not heard. Some men listened to a woman public speaker because she was a curiosity. Others listened because they wanted to jeer at the woman's words. A few rowdies even pelted the speaker with mud.

At first the campaign did little to change the attitudes of men. But it did start to move women to

new thoughts and actions. The women's rights
workers began telling other women they could
achieve power through the vote. And women began
to listen.

Throughout the 1850s women's rights workers
fought for the vote. They lived on the few dollars
that had been donated to the cause. The women tra-
veled, usually alone, to far-flung towns and villages.
There they knocked on doors and tried to hold public
meetings. Doors slammed in front of them, and only
a handful of people attended each of their meetings.

The woman suffrage work ground to a halt when the United States exploded into a bloody Civil War. During the fury of a war no one wanted to listen to a group of women demanding the vote.

When peace came, several new amendments were added to the United States Constitution. Those amendments gave voting rights to the newly freed slaves. At first the women's rights workers applauded these amendments. But Susan B. Anthony was shocked when she read the proposal for the Fourteenth Amendment to the Constitution. It read: "But when the right to vote. . . is denied to any male inhabitant of such state. . . . "

Male! An amendment guaranteeing males the right to vote was about to be put into the Constitution. Even the original Constitution did not mention the word male when granting the right to vote. Instead, the Constitution let the states determine who could or could not vote.

Led by Miss Anthony, the women's rights workers returned to their campaign. The Civil War was over, but they waged a new war for an amendment that would give the right to vote to half the country—the women.

In 1869 the woman suffrage movement gained

some organization, but lost some unity. The leadership divided over how to achieve the vote. Susan B. Anthony and Elizabeth Stanton formed an organization called the National Woman Suffrage Association. Its membership was open only to women. Its goal was to pass an amendment to the United States Constitution giving women the vote. Lucy Stone formed a separate organization called the American Woman Suffrage Association. Its membership was open to both men and women, and its goal was for women to gain the right to vote in state elections. Mrs. Stone's organization was more conservative than the one headed by Miss Anthony and Mrs. Stanton. The two suffrage organizations fought separate wars, and did not unite for the next twenty years.

While the women's organizations were campaigning in the East, a minor miracle was brewing in the western Territory of Wyoming.

Wyoming. The name rings with feelings of the Old West where men were men and rough, tough cowboys ruled. Yet Wyoming was the first government in the United States to give women the unreserved right to vote. Some historians say that Wyoming granted suffrage in order to attract more women to the territory. Wyoming passed the act in 1869 when men in the territory outnumbered women six to one.

Certainly an important figure in Wyoming's woman suffrage act was a hard-driving woman named Esther Morris. Mrs. Morris was a hardy, six-foot-tall western settler. She became a women's rights worker after listening to a speech by Susan B. Anthony. Soon after hearing the speech, Mrs. Morris convinced a male friend to introduce the suffrage bill. Esther Morris later became a Justice of the Peace, and one story tells of her throwing her own husband into jail for being drunk.

ELIZABETH CADY STANTON

SUSAN B. ANTHONY

ESTHER MORRIS

When Wyoming became a state in 1889, it retained its woman suffrage laws. Three other western states followed Wyoming's lead. In 1893 Colorado gave women the vote. In 1896 both Utah and Idaho passed woman suffrage laws. Frontier women usually did the same back-breaking work as men. So it was not surprising that western states led the country in granting woman suffrage. But after Utah and Idaho, no other state granted women the right to vote for the next fourteen years. Meanwhile, the pioneers of the women's rights movement were growing old.

None of the famous four of women's rights lived to see the suffrage amendment added to the Constitution. Lucretia Mott, the oldest founder of the movement, died in 1880. Lucy Stone died in 1893. Much of her work was taken over by her daughter, Alice Stone Blackwell. Elizabeth Stanton died in 1902.

Susan B. Anthony was the last living founder of the women's rights movement. She died the way she had lived—full of fight. At the age of eighty-five, Miss Anthony crossed the continent to attend a suffrage convention in Oregon. At eighty-six she attended a convention in Baltimore. There she pointed to her audience and said: "The fight must not cease. You must see it does not stop!" The audience, mostly young women, stood and applauded her for ten minutes.

On her last birthday, President Theodore Roosevelt sent Miss Anthony a telegram offering his congratulations. Feisty to the end, Susan Anthony said, "When will men do something besides extend congratulations? I would rather have President Roosevelt say one word to Congress in favor of amending the Constitution to give women the suffrage than to praise me endlessly." A few weeks later Susan B. Anthony died.

With the deaths of the founders, the torch of leadership passed to a new generation of woman suffrage workers. They were often called suffragists. These younger women were impatient with the slow methods of the past. By the turn of the century, the woman suffrage movement was fifty years old. But only four small states had granted women the vote.

With their banners held high, the suffragists held parades and rallies. Sometimes they broke laws and went to jail. But slowly the suffragists achieved results. The state of Washington granted equal suffrage to women in 1910. Washington was followed by California in 1911, and Kansas and Oregon in 1912. In 1913 Illinois granted women the right to vote in presidential elections. It was the first state east of the Mississippi to allow women limited voting privileges. The movement won its greatest victory in 1917 when the state of New York granted equal suffrage to women.

By 1917 sixteen states had granted women some form of the vote. The suffragists were proud of their gains, but it was clear they needed a victory on a national scale. Many states had given women only partial suffrage. States in the deep South had given no suffrage to women. The suffragists would not rest until the Constitution was amended to give every woman in the country an equal vote in every election.

An amendment granting women the vote had been proposed several times in the past. Such an amendment was introduced to the United States Senate in 1878. The Senate rejected the proposal. Over the years the woman suffrage amendment became known as the "Anthony Amendment," after Susan B. Anthony. The amendment was again defeated in the Senate in 1887. In order for an amendment to become a law it must be approved by a two-thirds majority in the Senate, and a two-thirds majority in the House of Representatives. Then it must be approved by two-thirds of the states. The Anthony Amendment was introduced a third time to the Senate in 1914. With the amendment, the suffragists presented the senators a petition signed by 500,000 men and women urging approval. The petition did little good. Again the Senate defeated the Anthony Amendment.

While the struggle for the voting rights amendment continued, the United States became entangled in World War I. With so many men fight-

ing overseas, a host of new jobs opened up to women. The suffrage parades continued, but suddenly the women marching in the parades were not simply schoolteachers or college seniors. Now the parading women wore coveralls from the late-night shift at the airplane factory. Women also drove trucks and streetcars and operated freight elevators. These women, working side by side with men, put an end to the absurd argument that women were not equal to men and therefore did not deserve the vote.

Two of the new generation of woman suffrage leaders were Carrie Chapman Catt and Alice Paul. Mrs. Catt was a gifted politician. She was president of the National American Woman Suffrage Association, which was formed when the two earlier suffrage organizations combined. Male politicians had to respect Mrs. Catt because of the growing power of women voters. Alice Paul took a more direct approach to accomplishing her goals. She took the cause of the Anthony Amendment directly to the streets. Miss Paul believed the Anthony Amendment would pass if the president of the United States came out strongly for it.

When Woodrow Wilson became president in 1913 he was greeted by a spectacular parade of some

eight thousand women marching past the White House. Leading the parade was Alice Paul. This was just the beginning of her campaign. President Wilson said he favored woman suffrage, but was opposed to the Anthony Amendment. Alice Paul and a determined band of women decided to picket the

White House until the president changed his mind.
During the war years the pickets were called "trai-
tors" and "turncoats" by people on the street. In
1917 Miss Paul was arrested on the White House
steps, and sentenced to seven months in jail. Miss
Paul carried her protest into jail by refusing to eat.

Finally President Wilson reversed his stand and came out in favor of the Anthony Amendment. Events moved quickly after Wilson's declaration. The very next day the amendment passed the House of Representatives. In June of 1919, the Senate approved the Anthony Amendment. The suffragists then carried their campaign to the state legislatures. They needed the approval of thirty-six states. On August 18, 1920, Tennessee became the thirty-sixth state to approve. Eight days later the Nineteenth Amendment to the Constitution became the law of the land.

After almost a century of struggle, women had won the right to vote.

Some critics said that women voting would ruin the country. But history proved the critics wrong. Today an amendment called ERA (Equal Rights Amendment) is being considered by state legislatures. The amendment is designed to assure American women total equality with men. Again some critics are saying the ERA would ruin the country. Once more, history probably will prove them wrong.

In 1920 the battle for woman suffrage ended. Many suffragists said a prayer for the founders of

EQUALITY OF RIGHTS UNDER THE LAW SHALL NOT BE DENIED OR ABRIDGED BY THE UNITED STATES OR BY ANY STATE ON ACCOUNT OF SEX.

their movement. In the face of jeers, insults, and ignorance those founders continued their fight. The Nineteenth Amendment is a monument to the courage of Lucy Stone, Elizabeth Stanton, Lucretia Mott, Susan B. Anthony, and hundreds of other women.

In the fall of 1920, millions of women registered to vote in their first nationwide election. Suffragist Carrie Chapman Catt said: "Women have suffered an agony of soul... that you and your daughters might inherit political freedom. That vote has been costly. *Prize it!*"

About the Author

R. Conrad Stein was born and grew up in Chicago. He enlisted in the Marine Corps at the age of eighteen and served for three years. He then attended the University of Illinois where he received a bachelor's degree in history. He later studied in Mexico, earning an advanced degree from the University of Guanajuato. Mr. Stein is the author of many other books, articles, and short stories written for young people.

Mr. Stein now lives in Pennsylvania with his wife, Deborah Kent, who is also a writer of books for young readers.

About the Artist

Keith Neely attended the School of the Art Institute of Chicago and received a Bachelor of Fine Arts degree with honors from the Art Center College of Design, where he majored in illustration. He has worked as an art director, designer, and illustrator and has taught advertising illustration and advertising design at Biola College in La Mirada, California. Mr. Neely is currently a freelance illustrator whose work has appeared in numerous magazines, books, and advertisements. He lives with his wife and five children in Flossmoor, Illinois, a suburb of Chicago.